GRADE
3

ReadyGEN

Text Collection

PEARSON

Glenview, Illinois • Boston, Massachusetts • Chandler, Arizona • Hoboken, New Jersey

ISBN-13: 978-0-328-78845-3
ISBN-10:   0-328-78845-7
2 3 4 5 6 7 8 9 10 V004 18 17 16 15 14

Table of Contents

Unit 4 Becoming an Active Citizen

Knots
on a Counting Rope

By Bill Martin Jr. and John Archambault
Illustrated by Ted Rand

Tell me the story again, Grandfather.
Tell me who I am.
    I have told you many times, Boy.
    You know the story by heart.
But it sounds better
when you tell it, Grandfather.
    Then listen carefully.
    This may be the last telling.
No, no, Grandfather.
There will never be a last time.
Promise me that.
Promise me.
    I promise you nothing, Boy.
    I love you.
    That is better than a promise.
And I love you, Grandfather,
but tell me the story again.
Please.

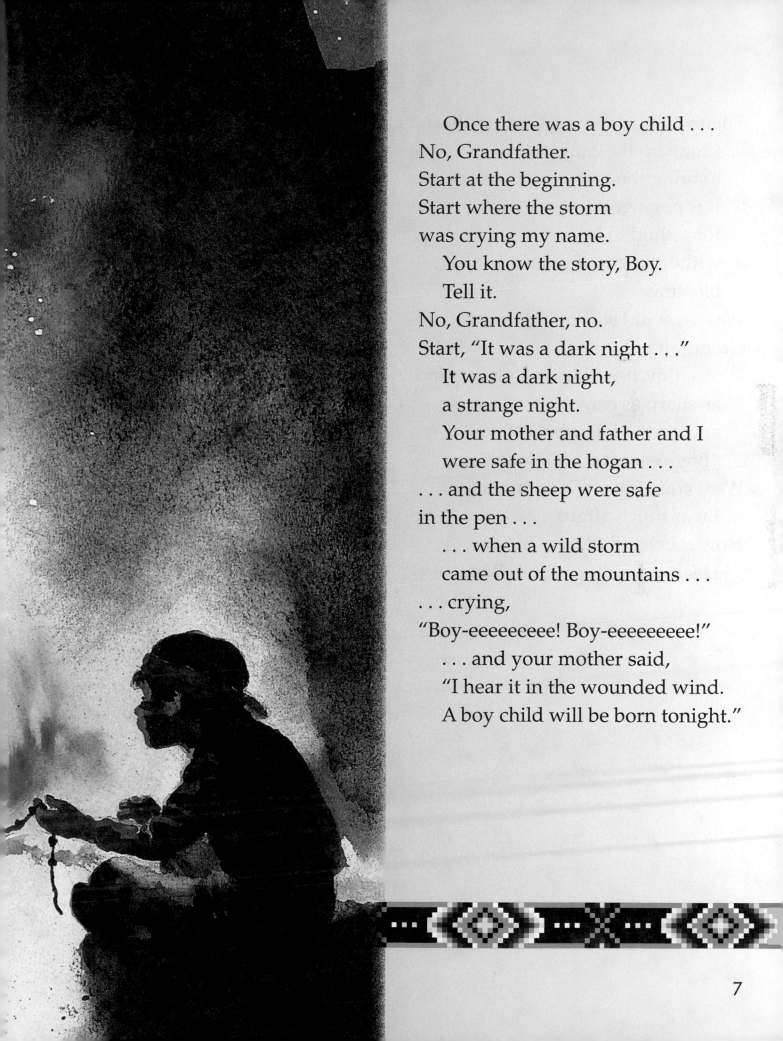

Once there was a boy child . . .
No, Grandfather.
Start at the beginning.
Start where the storm
was crying my name.
    You know the story, Boy.
    Tell it.
No, Grandfather, no.
Start, "It was a dark night . . ."
    It was a dark night,
    a strange night.
    Your mother and father and I
    were safe in the hogan . . .
. . . and the sheep were safe
in the pen . . .
    . . . when a wild storm
    came out of the mountains . . .
. . . crying,
"Boy-eeeeeeeee! Boy-eeeeeeeee!"
    . . . and your mother said,
    "I hear it in the wounded wind.
    A boy child will be born tonight."

Then what happened, Grandfather?
   I rode up the canyon fast,
   to bring the grandmother.
   It is not a good sign
   for a child to be born
   without a grandmother's
   blessing.
Was the wind still calling for me,
Grandfather?
   Yes, Boy, it was whipping up sand
   as sharp as claws,
   and crying like a bobcat,
   "Boy-eeeeeeeee! Boy-eeeeeeeee!"
Were you afraid, Grandfather?
   I was much afraid.
How much afraid?
   Heart-pounding afraid, Boy.

Then what happened, Grandfather?
Just as I was born . . .
tell me that part.
    It was strange . . . strange.
    Just as you came forth
    and made your first cry,
    the wind stopped howling
    and the storm was over . . .
. . . and the night became as quiet
as soft falling snow . . .
    . . . The grandmother took you up
    in her arms, and said,
    "He will walk in beauty . . .
    to the east . . ."
". . . to the west,
to the north, to the south,
he will walk in beauty. . ."
    ". . . forever."
And I was born strong,
wasn't I, Grandfather?
    No, you were not strong.
    You were sick and frail.
    We thought you would die.
But I didn't die, did I?
Tell me about that, Grandfather.

All night you lay silent
with your eyes closed,
your breath too shallow,
too weak for crying . . .
. . . and you carried me out
to see the morning, Grandfather,
but I did not open my eyes.
Tell me that part.

   Two great blue horses
   came galloping by . . .
. . . and they stopped, Grandfather!
They stopped and looked at me . . .

     . . . and you raised your arms
     to the great blue horses,
     and I said,
     "See how the horses speak to him.
     They are his brothers from . . . "
". . . from beyond the dark mountains.
This boy child will not die."
That is what you said,
isn't it, Grandfather?

     Yes, Boy, that is what I said,
     "This boy child will not die.
     The great blue horses have given
     him the strength to live."

And that is when you named me,
isn't it, Grandfather?
    After you smiled your first smile,
    we had the naming ceremony.
    All of the grandmothers
    and grandfathers were there.
And you named me
Boy-Strength-of-Blue-Horses.
    It is a strong name.
Did I need a strong name,
Grandfather?
    All children need a strong name
    to help them grow strong.
And I grew strong, didn't I?
    Yes, Boy-Strength-of-Blue-Horses,
    and each day
    you are growing stronger.
    You are learning to cross
    the dark mountains.

I already have crossed
some of the dark mountains.
    There will be more, Boy.
    Dark mountains
    are always around us.
    They have no beginnings and . . .
. . . they have no endings.
But we know they are there,
Grandfather, when we suddenly
feel afraid.
    Yes, Boy . . . afraid to do
    what we have to do.
Will I always have to live in the
dark?
    Yes, Boy.
    You were born with a dark
    curtain in front of your eyes.
But there are many ways to see,
Grandfather.
    Yes, Boy, you are learning
    to see through your darkness
    because you have
    the strength of blue horses.

I see the horses with my hands,
Grandfather,
but I cannot see the blue.
What is *blue?*
    You know *morning*, Boy.
Yes, I can feel *morning.*
Morning throws off
the blanket of night.
    And you know *sunrise.*
Yes, I hear *sunrise,*
in the song of the birds.
    And you know *sky*, Boy.
Yes, *sky* touches my face . . .
soft, like lambs' wool . . .
and I breathe its softness.
    Blue is all of these.
    Blue is the feeling
    of a spring day beginning.
    Try . . . try to see it, Boy.
Blue?. . . blue?
Blue is the morning . . .
the sunrise . . .
the sky . . .
the song of the birds . . .
O, I see it!
Blue! Blue!
Blue is happiness, Grandfather!
I feel it . . .
in my heart!

There was a sweep of blue
in the rainbow, Boy,
that morning your horse was born.
O, tell me that part, Grandfather!
I could not see the rainbow
but I can still feel its happiness.
   I awakened you, Boy,
   during the night, remember,
   just before the foal was born.
And you said to me,
"Come, Boy,
Circles is ready to foal.
The colt will be yours."
   It was a long night of cold rain . . .
. . . and we put a blanket
over Circles, Grandfather,
to keep her warm.
   Yes, Boy.
   As the sun
   came through the clouds,
   the foal was born . . .
. . . and a rainbow
danced across the sky.
   It was a good sign, Boy.
And I named the little wet foal . . .
Rainbow!
   You have trained her well, Boy.
Rainbow is smart, Grandfather.
   Like you.
   She is good at remembering.

Rainbow is my eyes, Grandfather.
She takes me to the sheep,
wherever they are,
and when I am ready,
she finds the way home.
 No one thought you could teach her
 to race, Boy . . .
. . . but I did, Grandfather!
Every day, day after day,
we followed you along the trail . . .
And you let me hold the reins.
 You traced the trails
 in your mind, Boy,
 both you and Rainbow.
Yes, Grandfather,
we learned the trails by heart . . .
up South Mountain to Granite Rock . . .
down the steep shortcut
to Meadow-of-Blue-Flowers . . .
then straight across the Red Flats
to Lightning-Split-Tree . . .
then down the Switchbacks
to the canyon trail . . .
and on around to the finish line.
I learned from Rainbow when to turn
by the pull of her neck
and by counting her gallops.
Now tell me again about the race,
Grandfather.

It was a tribal day, Boy.
You and the other boys
were at the starting line . . .
but you pulled back.
I was afraid, Grandfather,
until you called to me.
Tell me again what you said.
    I said,
    "Don't be afraid, Boy!
    Trust your darkness!
    Go like the wind!"
And I leaned forward
on Rainbow's neck.
I grabbed her mane tight,
and I said, "Go, Rainbow, go!"
I could feel the
pushing and crowding
and galloping thunder
all around me.
Rainbow and I
went twisting, turning,
galloping, galloping, galloping,
counting the gallops . . .
remembering the way . . .
And what did the people say,
Grandfather?
    They said,
    "Who is that boy riding bareback . . .
    racing the race with all of his heart?"

And you said,
"That is Boy-Strength-of-Blue-Horses . . .
He and his horse are together like one."
    Yes, Boy, that is what I said.
But I didn't win, Grandfather.
    No, but you rode like the wind.
The wind is my friend, Grandfather.
It throws back my hair
and laughs in my face.
    You see the wind better than I, Boy.
I finished the race, hot and dusty,
sweat dripping from my face . . .
    And you were smiling, Boy!
I wasn't afraid, Grandfather.
I could see through the dark
every turn of the race.
Rainbow and I knew the way.
    You were crossing dark mountains, Boy!
Tell me again what you told me then.
I like to hear it over and over.
    I said,
    "Boy-Strength-of-Blue-Horses,
    you have raced darkness and won!
    You now can see with your heart,
    feel a part of all that surrounds you.
    Your courage lights the way."
And what did the grandmothers say?
    You tell me, Boy.
    I know you remember.
Yes, I remember, Grandfather.

They said,
"This boy walks in beauty.
His dreams are more beautiful
than rainbows and sunsets."
     Now, Boy . . .
     now that the story has been told
     again,
     I will tie another knot
     in the counting rope.
     When the rope is filled with knots,
     you will know the story by heart
     and can tell it to yourself.
So that I will grow stronger,
Grandfather?
     Yes . . . stronger . . . strong enough
     to cross the dark mountains.
I always feel strong when you are with
me, Grandfather.
     I will not always be with you, Boy.
No, Grandfather,
don't ever leave me.
What will I do without you?
     You will never be alone, Boy.
     My love will always surround you . . .
     with the strength of blue horses.

PAUL BUNYAN

adapted by STEPHEN KRENSKY

illustrations by CRAIG ORBACK

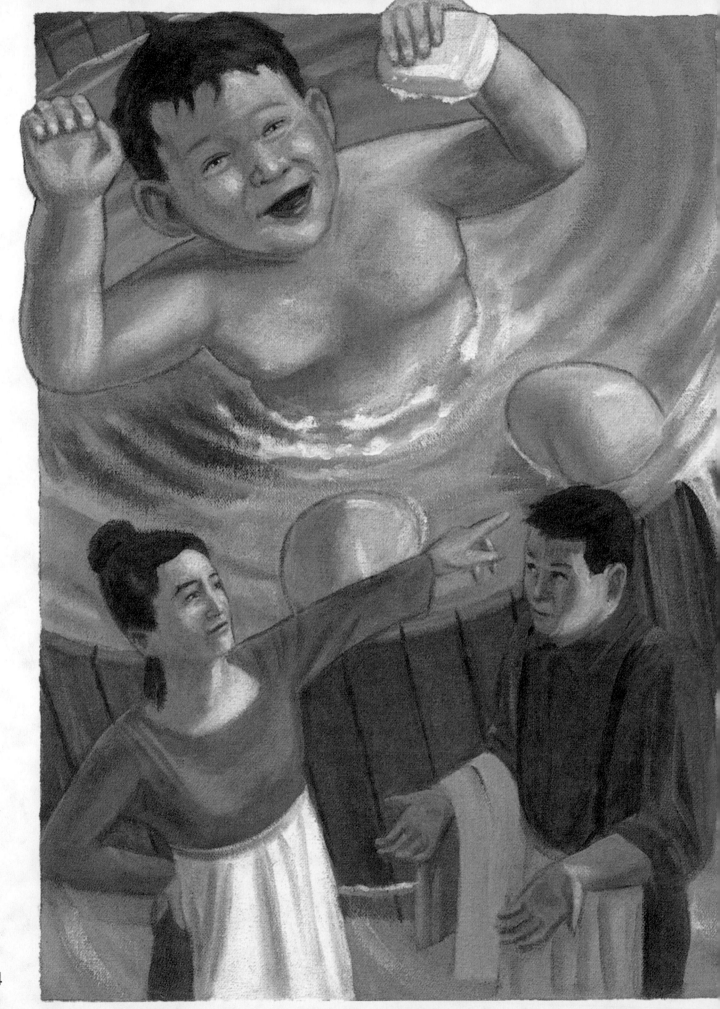

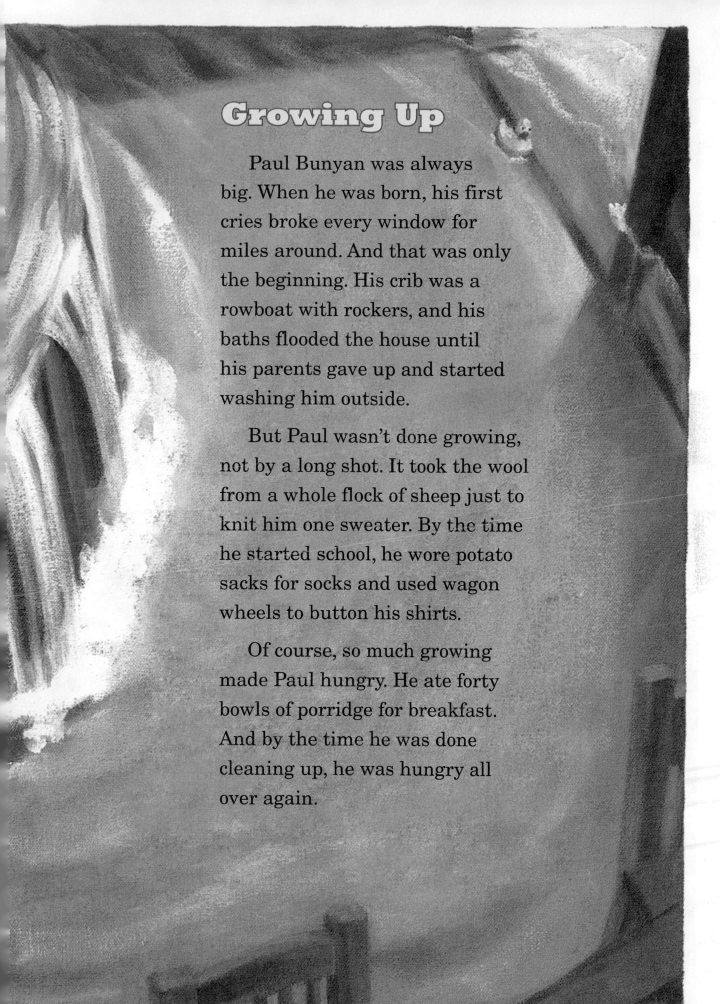

Growing Up

Paul Bunyan was always big. When he was born, his first cries broke every window for miles around. And that was only the beginning. His crib was a rowboat with rockers, and his baths flooded the house until his parents gave up and started washing him outside.

But Paul wasn't done growing, not by a long shot. It took the wool from a whole flock of sheep just to knit him one sweater. By the time he started school, he wore potato sacks for socks and used wagon wheels to button his shirts.

Of course, so much growing made Paul hungry. He ate forty bowls of porridge for breakfast. And by the time he was done cleaning up, he was hungry all over again.

When Paul was fifteen, the winter was so cold even the snow turned blue. One morning, Paul found a young ox half-buried in a snowdrift. If that wasn't odd enough, the ox was as blue as the snow itself. "My poor little babe," he said. And that's how Babe got his name. Paul never found out where Babe came from. But it didn't matter. Paul was just happy to have a new friend.

Babe was really strong. In one of their first jobs, Paul hitched him up to a crooked road that needed fixing. "Pull!" he said. And Babe pulled. The road was pretty stubborn, but so were Paul and Babe. By the time the sun set, they had that road straightened out just fine. "Good work!" Paul said to Babe, and Babe snorted back. They made a good team.

27

Starting Out

Paul was always comfortable holding an ax. With his very first swing, he cut down a half-grown pine tree. He used it to brush his hair until the needles fell out.

When he got older, Paul decided to be a lumberjack. At first, he had only Babe to help him. Paul cut down the trees, and Babe pulled them into stacks beside the river.

But there was more work to be done, more than even Paul and Babe could do. So Paul hired himself a crew. His most famous workers were his seven axmen—all named Elmer. Each Elmer weighed over 300 pounds and was over six feet tall sitting down. The Elmers didn't chop wood with regular axes. They worked faster twirling the blades around them.

Sourdough Sam, the cook, fed Paul's logging crews. Sam's soup kettle was so big, he had to row a boat out to the center. At dinner, his cookhouse boys wore roller skates to get from one end of the dining tables to the other.

The axmen ate hundreds of flapjacks. Sourdough Sam was always running out of space to make them. So, Ole the Blacksmith made a new griddle. A dozen men skated on bacon slabs to grease it. At first, the flapjacks in the middle were too hard to reach. Then Sam added popcorn to the batter so the flapjacks flipped themselves.

The Year of the Two Winters

It was always cold in the winter. The lumberjacks were used to that. But one year was much colder than the rest. Maybe Paul should have seen it coming. The leaves that fall didn't turn red or yellow. They turned dark blue from the cold.

Once the snow started falling, it just wouldn't quit. At first, the lumberjacks cut new paths through the fresh snow every day. But after a while, they let the snow pile up and dug tunnels under it instead.

After a month, the snow got so deep Paul had to dig down just to find the treetops.

Looking back, they called it the Year of the Two Winters. By January, the icicles had reached the ground and started to take root. Shadows froze against walls and couldn't get loose. Lucy the cow's milk turned to ice cream before it hit the pail. And lighting fires was no good because the flames froze solid. They were pretty to look at but weren't worth a lick for warmth.

Of course, things weren't all bad.
It was so cold even the
bedbugs huddled
together to keep warm.
Scooping them up was
quick and easy, so the lumberjacks
had clean sheets for once. Nobody
got any work done because keeping
warm was pretty much a full-time job.
The lumberjacks let their beards grow
and grow and grow. They wrapped them
around like scarves.

Even the snowmen needed more clothes than usual. When spring came, Paul cut everyone's beard. The whiskers were stacked up and later stuffed into mattresses. The cracking of the ice went on for weeks. The only people who got any sleep wore three pairs of earmuffs to bed. But nobody complained. They were just glad things were back to normal.

Moving On

Paul and Babe were happy the long winter was over. After being cooped up for so long, they were eager to stretch their legs. Paul hitched a plow to Babe, and they dug a groove from Round Lake down to the Gulf of Mexico. As the water rushed south, it made a nice wide river. Paul called it the Mississippi. He piled the dirt neatly on one side. There were a lot of stones and boulders mixed in. When he was done, he called the whole pile the Rocky Mountains.

On their way back north, Paul and Babe walked through the desert. It was terribly hot, and Paul took to dragging his great ax behind him. The heavy ax cut deeply into the soft sand. At sunset, Paul turned to look behind him. "What a grand canyon!" Paul said, and the name stuck after that.

Paul and his lumberjacks kept so busy that one day there were no more trees worth cutting down. Some of the loggers liked the look of the cleared land and decided to settle down. But not Paul. He needed more elbow room. So he and Babe said good-bye to the loggers and headed out west.

No one knows where they ended up, and Paul was careful not to leave any footprints behind. But every time you see a big mountain or a deep canyon or a rushing river, you know these things don't happen by themselves. So it's a pretty good bet that Paul Bunyan was there before you.

Arctic

Alberta, Canada
New York City, U.S.A.
Louisiana Bayou, U.S.A.
Texas Panhandle, U.S.A.
Barbados
Paris, France
Xian, China
Darjeeling, India
Thailand
Dakar, Senegal
Nile Valley, Egypt
Kenya
Amazon Basin, Brazil
Darwin, Australia
Patagonia, Argentina
Antarctica

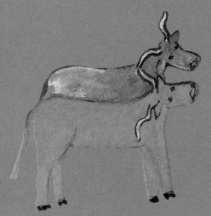

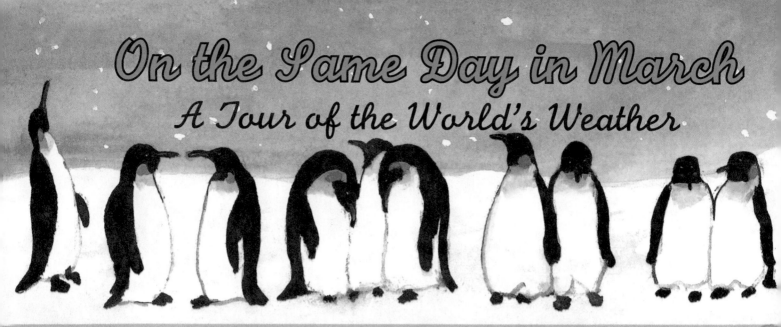

On the Same Day in March
A Tour of the World's Weather

Marilyn Singer • illustrated by Frané Lessac

In the Arctic

Polar bears ride on floes of ice,
stalking seals,
wishing fish,
as the six-month sun begins to rise
slowly in the Arctic skies.

On the same day in March . . .

in *Alberta, Canada*

Just when you can't even remember spring,
that wild chinook blows in like a dragon,
and quicker than you can say Medicine Hat,
the biggest snow fort ever
is nothing but a dragon-shaped patch
in somebody's backyard.

On the same day in March . . .

in *Paris, France*

The sun slips out, still winter pale.
But all over the city,
at bus stops and markets,
on small streets and grand boulevards,
people hurrying to work or school,
people, huddled in their coats and scarves,
sitting at outdoor cafés and sipping *chocolat*—
all of them turn up their faces
to enjoy the sun's shy smile.

On the same day in March . . .

in New York City

It's too gray to play outside today.
The parents sigh, the little kids complain.
But the basketball players stay in the school yard,
arguing what's worse—
snow or sleet or freezing rain.

On the same day in March . . .

in the **Texas Panhandle**

They said it was just a tiny twister—
not big enough to spin a horse
or hoist a cow.
But it did suck up a bucket of water
and give Grandma's dirty old truck
the first wash it's had in weeks.

On the same day in March . . .

48

49

in Darjeeling, India

Hailstones all over the hillside!
No one is happy
except little sister,
who thinks the moon has broken and scattered
its necklace of pearls.

On the same day in March . . .

50

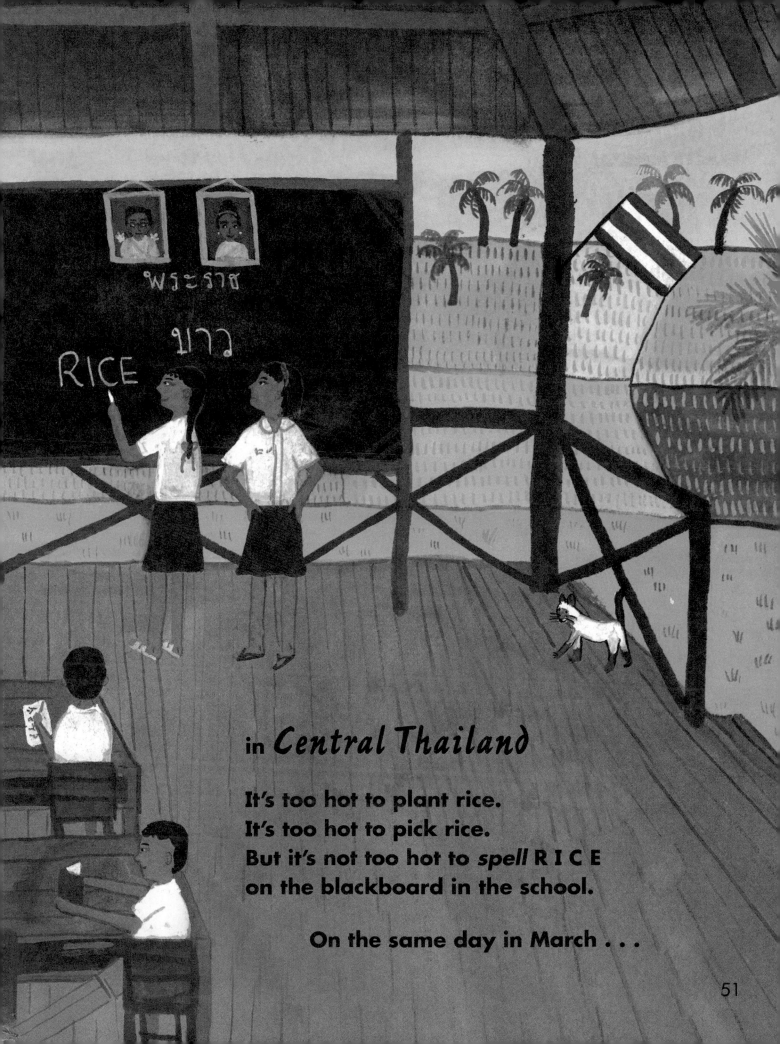

in *Central Thailand*

It's too hot to plant rice.
It's too hot to pick rice.
But it's not too hot to *spell* R I C E
on the blackboard in the school.

On the same day in March . . .

51

in Northern Kenya

The rains come,
and all in one day,
they leave the gift of a river.
Everyone, hurry!
Come drink! Come play!
Before the sun shines
and, all in one day,
takes the river away.

On the same day in March . . .

in Darwin, Australia

Board up the windows!
Bring in the boat!
Better to be like crocodiles crouched on the shore
than to be out sailing the sea
when the willy-willies come to call.

On the same day in March . . .

53

in Patagonia, Argentina

Over the wide, dry plain
autumn shears the clouds like a flock of sheep.
"Catch the wool," Mama teases her youngest son.
He doesn't understand why these white puffs
vanish wet and cold in his fat warm hands.

On the same day in March . . .

in **Antarctica**

Penguins scramble on the shore,
seeking mates,
missing fish,
as the six-month sun begins to slice
down below the Antarctic ice.

All on the same day in March!

A Note from the Author

It takes the earth 365 days—one year—to make a complete trip around the sun. The earth does not sit straight up and down in the heavens. It tilts on its axis—an imaginary line running through the center. The top of the axis is the North Pole; the bottom is the South Pole. As the earth orbits, sometimes the North Pole tips toward the sun, and sometimes it tips away from the sun. This tilt is what gives us the seasons.

In March, winter turns to spring in the Northern Hemisphere, and summer turns to fall in the Southern Hemisphere. The North Pole will soon lean closer to the sun, giving the Arctic six months of daylight and warmer weather. The South Pole will lean farther and farther away from the sun, slipping Antarctica into six months of darkness and bitter cold. On any given day in March, somewhere in the world, it may be raining, snowing, or hailing. It may be sunny, foggy, or windy.

There are places where the weather doesn't change much throughout the year. For example, in the equatorial rain forests, it is hot and humid and it does rain at the same time every day. There are other parts of the world where the weather can sometimes change from hour to hour. New York City, where I live, is one of those places.

Marilyn Singer

What Does the Thermometer Say?

There are two different scales used to measure temperature. If you live in the United States, temperature is measured on the Fahrenheit scale. If you live in a country that uses the metric system, temperature is measured on the Celsius scale. Look at this chart to see how the numbers measuring temperature are different.

hygrometer

Typical Temperatures

Celsius (°C)	Fahrenheit (°F)	Description
100	212	Water boils
40	104	Hot bath
37	98.6	Body temperature
30	86	Beach weather
21	70	Room temperature
10	50	Cool day
0	32	Freezing point of water
–18	0	Very cold day
–40	–40	Extremely cold day

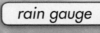

rain gauge

Tools for Measuring Weather

Scientists use a number of tools to help them measure and describe weather. These tools also help them predict what the weather will be like.

An anemometer measures wind speed. A wind vane shows the direction from which the wind is blowing. Both wind speed and direction affect the weather.

Scientists use a hygrometer to measure how much water vapor is in the air. The amount of water vapor in the air is called humidity. The humidity is low when air is dry. The humidity is high when air has more water vapor in it.

A rain gauge measures water too. A rain gauge measures how much rain has fallen.

Scientists can measure air pressure with a tool called a barometer. Changes in air pressure are clues to the kind of weather that is on the way. Low air pressure often means the weather will be cloudy or rainy. High air pressure often means fair weather with sunny, clear skies.

barometer

wind vane

anemometer

Where Would You Be?

by Karla Kuskin

Where would you be on a night like this
With the wind so dark and howling?
Close to the light
Wrapped warm and tight
Or there where the cats are prowling?

Where would you wish you on such a night
When the twisting trees are tossed?
Safe in a chair
In the lamp-lit air
Or out where the moon is lost?

Where would you be when the white waves roar
On the tumbling storm-torn sea?
Tucked inside
Where it's calm and dry
Or searching for stars in the furious sky
Whipped by the whine of the gale's wild cry
Out in the night with me?

Storm

by Adrien Stoutenberg

In a storm,
the wind talks
with its mouth wide open.
It yells around corners
with its eyes shut.
It bumps into itself
and falls over a roof
and whispers

OH . . . Oh . . . oh . . . .

The Wind

by James Reeves

I can get through a doorway without any key,
And strip the leaves from the great oak tree.

I can drive storm-clouds and shake tall towers,
Or steal through a garden and not wake the flowers.

Seas I can move and ships I can sink;
I can carry a house-top or the scent of pink.

When I am angry I can rave and riot;
And when I am spent, I lie quiet as quiet.

Tornado Season

by Adrien Stoutenberg

Wind went by with people falling out of it,
and hairpins,
and a barn door swinging without its hinges.
Grass rose in swarms along with nails.
A crow flew upsidedown,
his legs reaching skyward,
and growing longer.

Weather

Whether the weather be fine,
Or whether the weather be not,
Whether the weather be cold,
Or whether the weather be hot,
We'll weather the weather
Whatever the weather,
Whether we like it or not!

Anonymous

BACK OF THE BUS

BY AARON REYNOLDS
ILLUSTRATED BY FLOYD COOPER

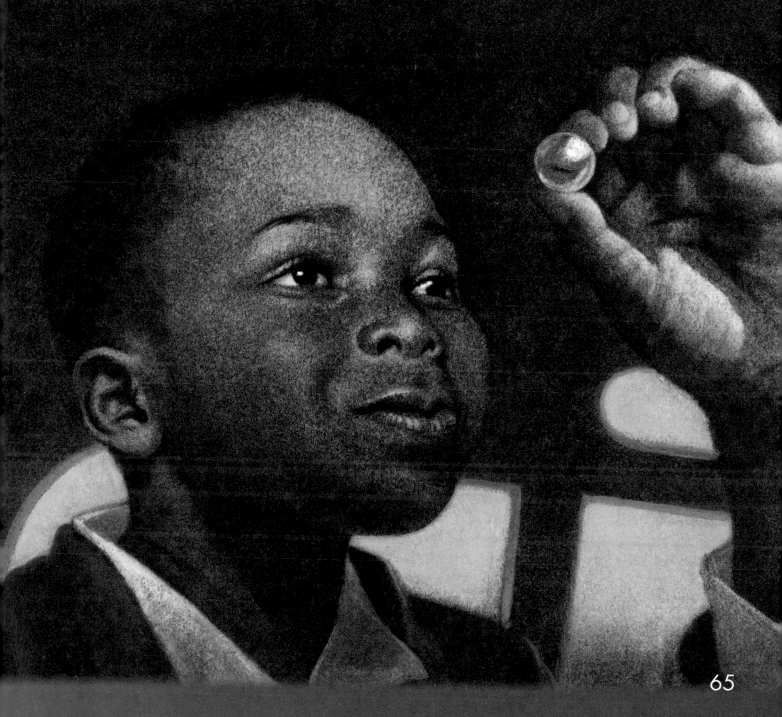

December 1, 1955
Montgomery, Alabama

Winter's here in Montgomery,
but I got the window down
and a warm breeze blowin' in
as Mama and me
huff down Cleveland Avenue
on the big ol' bus.

We're sittin' right where we're supposed to—
way in back.

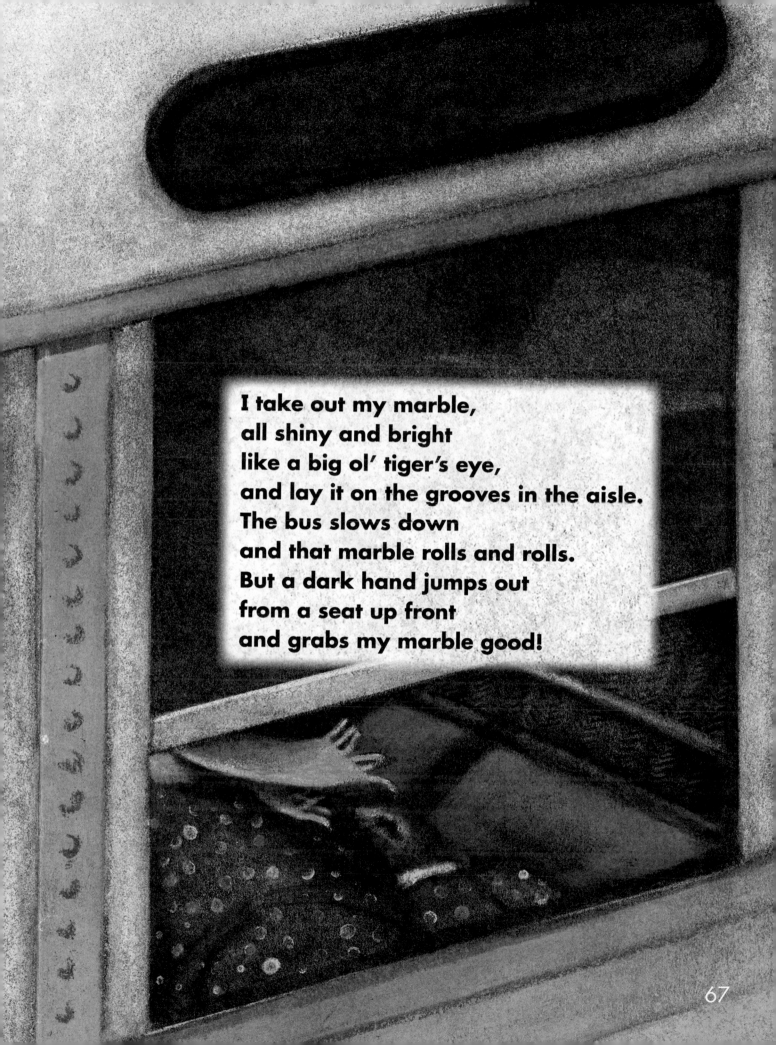

I take out my marble,
all shiny and bright
like a big ol' tiger's eye,
and lay it on the grooves in the aisle.
The bus slows down
and that marble rolls and rolls.
But a dark hand jumps out
from a seat up front
and grabs my marble good!

But it's just Mrs. Parks from the tailor shop.
She looks back, smilin', flings a wink at me,
and sets that marble back in its groove.
That bus takes off again
and my marble comes right back to me,
like I got it on a string.

Mama shakes "no" at me,
and I hold it snug in my hand.
She's got them worked-all-day eyes,
but she's got her strong chin on.

69

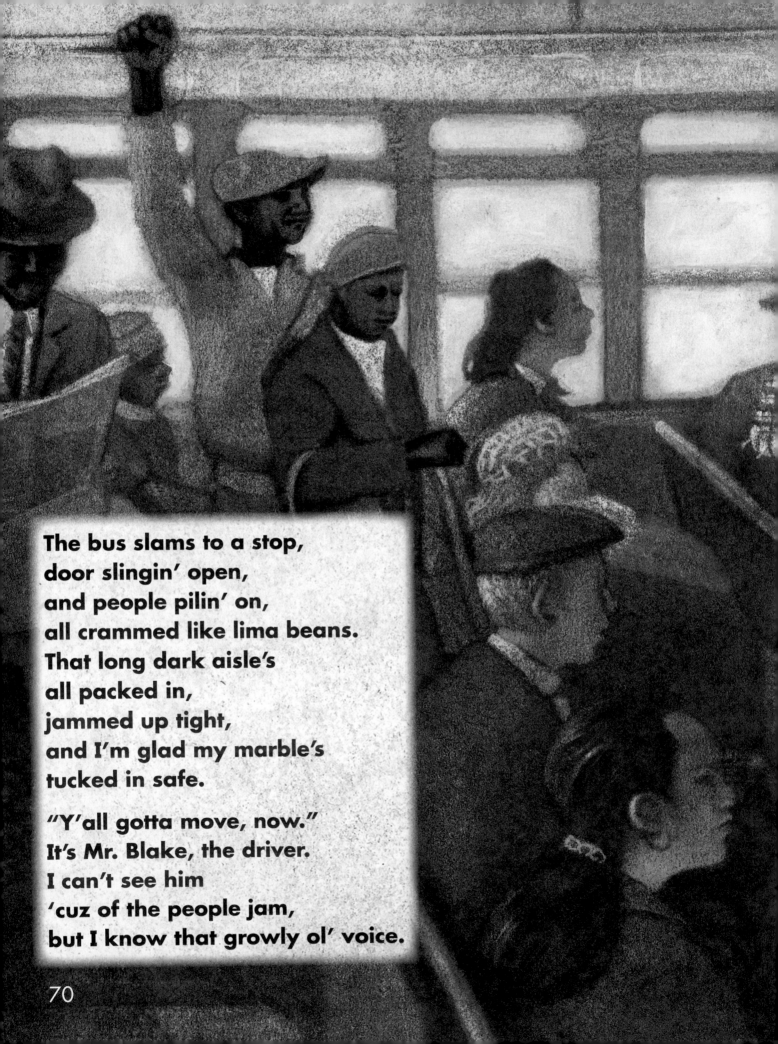

The bus slams to a stop,
door slingin' open,
and people pilin' on,
all crammed like lima beans.
That long dark aisle's
all packed in,
jammed up tight,
and I'm glad my marble's
tucked in safe.

"Y'all gotta move, now."
It's Mr. Blake, the driver.
I can't see him
'cuz of the people jam,
but I know that growly ol' voice.

Some folks get up, new ones sit down,
but still that bus is sittin' there stopped.
"Why ain't we goin', Mama?" I say all soft.
"Hush, child," she says.
And I do.

Somebody's talkin' back,
but I can't hear the words.
Just Mr. Blake sayin', "I'm gonna call the police, now."

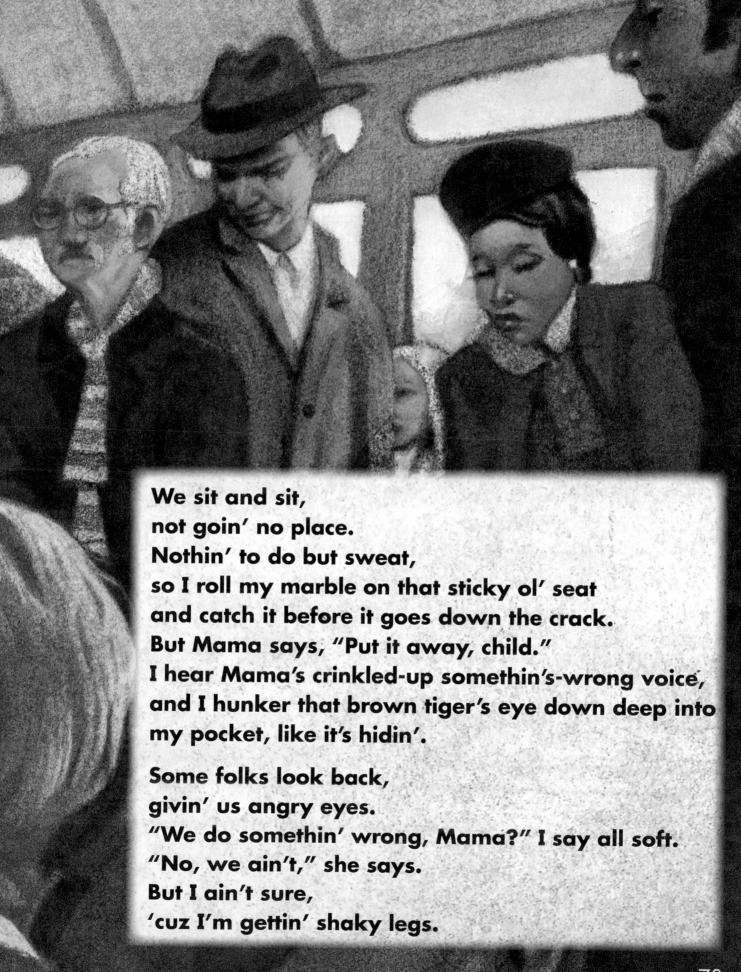

We sit and sit,
not goin' no place.
Nothin' to do but sweat,
so I roll my marble on that sticky ol' seat
and catch it before it goes down the crack.
But Mama says, "Put it away, child."
I hear Mama's crinkled-up somethin's-wrong voice,
and I hunker that brown tiger's eye down deep into
my pocket, like it's hidin'.

Some folks look back,
givin' us angry eyes.
"We do somethin' wrong, Mama?" I say all soft.
"No, we ain't," she says.
But I ain't sure,
'cuz I'm gettin' shaky legs.

Same folks are doin' mean scratchy whispers
at somebody sittin' up front.
And then I see who it is
from way in the back.
Mrs. Parks, that's who.
She don't belong up front like that,
and them folks all know it.
But she's sittin' right there,
her eyes all fierce like a lightnin' storm,
like maybe she does belong up there.
And I start thinkin' maybe she does too.

Fifteen whole minutes we sit,
but it feels like a big bunch more.
That breeze is long gone,
and I want me a drink real bad.
But then the policeman comes.

He walks right on my bus.
I'm all shaky inside now.
Them lima bean people spread aside,
and he stops at that way-up-front seat.

"Why won't you move and give this man your seat?"
he says to Mrs. Parks.
But she don't move.
She's just sittin' in that seat
like a turnip pile.
"I don't think I should have to stand up," she says.
"Why do you push us folks around?"
Her voice is all soft,
but she's got on her strong chin too, just like Mama's.

That policeman clicks them metal things on her hands,
quick and loud like the screen door slammin',
and off the bus they go.

More people sit,
and the air ain't warm no more.
She's gettin' hauled off to jail or worse,
and I'm watchin' out the window.
Mama too, with them long tired eyes.

"There you go, Rosa Parks, stirrin' up a nest of hornets,"
Mama's sayin' in her to-herself voice.
But I hear.
I see somethin' too—she's got Mrs. Parks' lightnin'-storm
eyes now.

"We in trouble, Mama?" I say all soft.
"No, we ain't," she says. "Don't you worry none.
Tomorrow all this'll be forgot."

But I got somethin' in me,
all pale and punchy,
sayin' it won't be.

Don't know why.
But instead of feelin' all shaky,
I feel a little strong.
Like Mama's chin.

I take out my marble
and I start to hide it in my squeezy-tight fist.
But instead, I hold it up to the light,
right out in the open.
That thing shines all brown and golden in the sunlight,
like it's smilin', I think.
'Cuz it ain't gotta hide no more.

Who Really Created Democracy?

by Amie Jane Leavitt

THE RACE

For thousands of years, people have been organizing into cities and countries. Their governments create rules to follow. But often wealthy people control how the countries are run. The poor have little or no power in the government.

In answer to this problem, democracy was born. In a democracy, people—rich and poor—make laws together. They also choose their own leaders. But where did this idea come from? Who created democracy? The race to democracy is long and difficult. The players are divided by centuries. But only one can be the winner. Who will it be?

MEET THE PLAYERS

AMERICAN COLONISTS

These people have settled in the 13 American colonies. By the 1770s, many colonists have lived in America their entire lives. But Great Britain still controls the colonies. Many colonists don't believe Great Britain treats America fairly.

ANCIENT GREEKS IN ATHENS

These people live in Athens in the fifth and fourth centuries BC. Most of the citizens are poor farmers who owe debts to the wealthy rulers of their city. They are frustrated and looking for change.

Trouble's Brewing

Life in Athens

Athens in 630 BC is a great city for the rich. The wealthy relax in comfortable homes. They own large plots of land and eat delicious food. And they make all of the laws for everyone else.

Only the rich are part of the oligarchy that rules Athens. Most Athenians are poor and struggle to grow crops on their tiny farms. They have to borrow money to buy food and pay taxes. They also have no say in Athens's laws.

Oligarchy: a government ruled by only a few people

The oligarchy's laws are very strict. If people can't pay their debts, they must sell family members into slavery. Families all over Athens are being separated this way. The poor are angry and frustrated.

At first, people just talk about their unhappiness. But soon, the talking grows to shouting. Then it grows to action. The poor begin to fight against wealthy rulers. Athens is no longer a peaceful city.

The poor outnumber the rich. The wealthy lawmakers know they can't fight the masses. But Athens is heading straight for a civil war. The rulers have to make changes to the government quickly. Is there any way to bring peace?

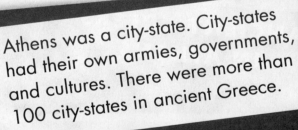

RACE FACT

Athens was a city-state. City-states had their own armies, governments, and cultures. There were more than 100 city-states in ancient Greece.

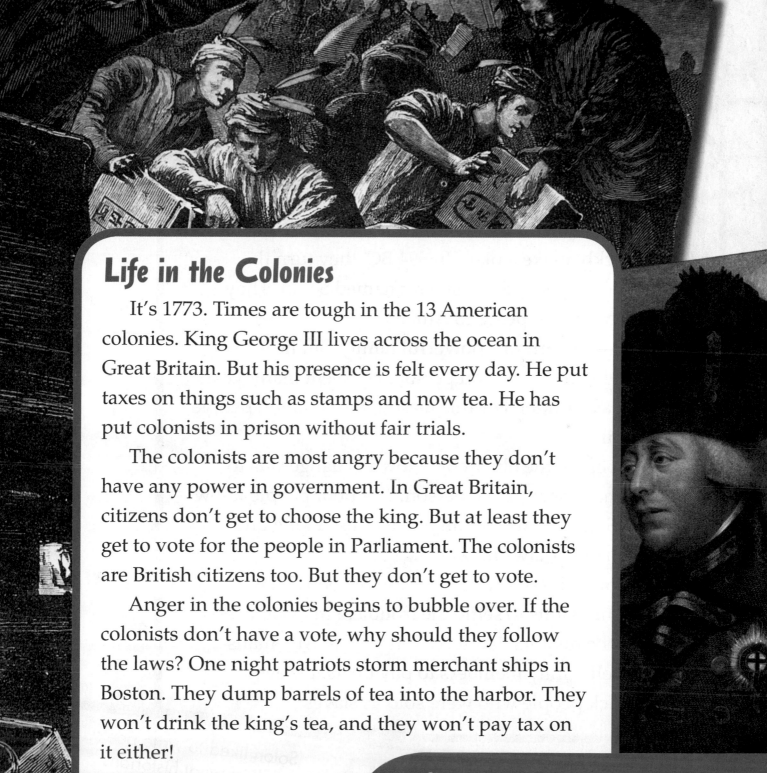

Life in the Colonies

It's 1773. Times are tough in the 13 American colonies. King George III lives across the ocean in Great Britain. But his presence is felt every day. He put taxes on things such as stamps and now tea. He has put colonists in prison without fair trials.

The colonists are most angry because they don't have any power in government. In Great Britain, citizens don't get to choose the king. But at least they get to vote for the people in Parliament. The colonists are British citizens too. But they don't get to vote.

Anger in the colonies begins to bubble over. If the colonists don't have a vote, why should they follow the laws? One night patriots storm merchant ships in Boston. They dump barrels of tea into the harbor. They won't drink the king's tea, and they won't pay tax on it either!

The king is furious. He makes even harsher laws. The colonists begin to whisper plans for war. The situation is quickly spinning out of control.

Parliament: the group of people who have been elected to make the laws in England

patriot: an American who disagreed with British rule

85

Big Decisions

Changing the Rule of Athens

The unrest in Athens is also spinning out of control. The wealthy rulers need to find a way to calm the city. They quickly make a plan. In 594 BC, they turn the government over to an aristocrat named Solon. They hope he can bring peace to Athens.

Solon was born to a powerful family. But he's also lived the life of a common person. He spent many years working as a trader. For this reason, the common people seem to like him.

Members of the oligarchy know it's dangerous to give all the power to one person. The poor people know it too. If Solon wants, he can make himself king and create whatever laws he wants.

But Solon doesn't want to abuse his power. He loves Athens and wants to settle the trouble. First, Solon changes the debtors' laws. No longer will Athenians have to sell family members to pay debts. He even brings back people who were sold as slaves.

RACE FACT Solon liked to write poetry. Much of what historians know about Solon comes from his poems.

aristocrat: a member of a group of people thought to be the best in some way, usually based on their wealth

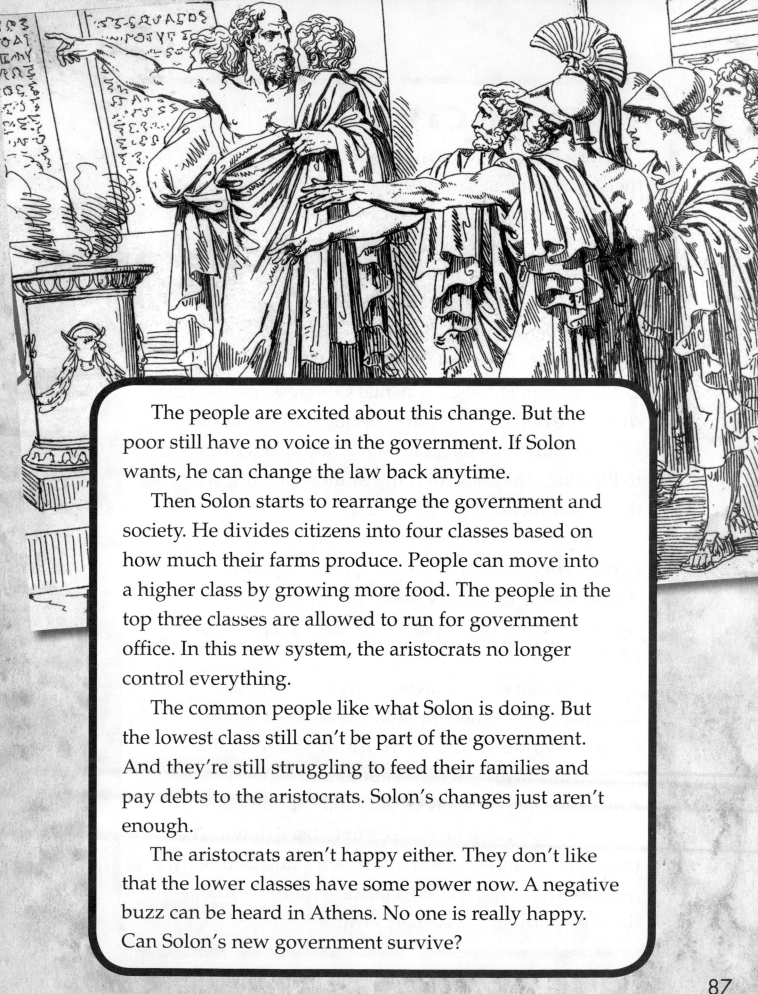

The people are excited about this change. But the poor still have no voice in the government. If Solon wants, he can change the law back anytime.

Then Solon starts to rearrange the government and society. He divides citizens into four classes based on how much their farms produce. People can move into a higher class by growing more food. The people in the top three classes are allowed to run for government office. In this new system, the aristocrats no longer control everything.

The common people like what Solon is doing. But the lowest class still can't be part of the government. And they're still struggling to feed their families and pay debts to the aristocrats. Solon's changes just aren't enough.

The aristocrats aren't happy either. They don't like that the lower classes have some power now. A negative buzz can be heard in Athens. No one is really happy. Can Solon's new government survive?

The Colonists Go to War

The American colonists continue to struggle with their government. The patriots hate Britain's unfair treatment of the colonies. But what can they do? After the Tea Party, Parliament closed Boston Harbor. British soldiers now march through the colonies. And the king just signed a bill that forces colonists to house and feed those soldiers.

Patriot leaders meet in Philadelphia in September 1774. Leaders at the Continental Congress discuss what should be done. Finally, they decide the colonies will stop all trade with Great Britain. They also write a letter to the king. They ask for fair treatment and a voice in the government.

The patriots' efforts only make the king and Parliament angrier. In April 1775, the king orders British troops to destroy the colonists' storage of weapons. Word of the plan leaks out. The patriots prepare to fight.

The British army marches toward Lexington, Massachusetts. When the soldiers arrive, a small band of patriots is waiting. A British officer orders the patriots to drop their weapons and leave. The Americans face an army of hundreds of trained soldiers. They have no choice but to back down. They turn to go, but they won't leave their guns. Suddenly, a gunshot rings out. A British officer orders his troops to fire. The patriots fire back. It's war!

The patriots fought the British at the Battle of Lexington on April 19, 1775.

RACE FACT Historians don't know which side fired the first shot that started the Revolutionary War.

Jefferson (standing) worked with other patriots like Benjamin Franklin (left) and John Adams (center) on the declaration.

In June 1776, patriot leaders ask Thomas Jefferson to write a declaration. They want to tell the world that they are fighting this war to be independent from Great Britain. In the document, Jefferson lists the ways the king has wronged the colonists. The king has refused to give them a say in the government. He has made them pay unfair taxes. He hasn't given the colonists fair trials. Jefferson writes that the colonists will no longer take this unjust treatment.

The document is presented to the patriot leaders on July 4, 1776. Fifty-six men sign their names to the Declaration of Independence. By doing so, they are committing treason against Great Britain. The king could have them killed for this act. Winning the war is now life or death for the colonists.

RACE FACT Two future presidents signed the declaration—John Adams and Thomas Jefferson.

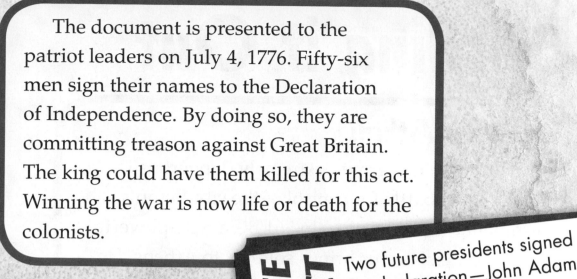

signing the Declaration of Independence

declaration: a public announcement
treason: the crime of betraying your country or government

Battling it Out

Fighting in Athens

The situation has grown extremely dangerous in Athens. People battle for control of the city. Solon's government cannot survive. In 561 BC a rich, powerful man named Peisistratus brings soldiers to Athens. He takes control of the government. Solon is old and weak. He warns that Peisistratus is a tyrant. But Peisistratus tells the people he was chosen by the god Athena. They agree to let him rule.

Peisistratus does many good things for Athens. He increases trade to the city. He also has channels built to bring water to Athens. But the people have no control over what Peisistratus does. He makes all the laws and rules the government.

In 527 BC, Peisistratus dies. His son Hippias takes control. Hippias is a cruel leader. He taxes the people for births and deaths. It's a tax few can afford. In 508 BC the aristocrats hire an army to remove Hippias from power. When he flees, another tyrant called Isagoras takes his place. The fighting continues until the aristocrats remove him from office too.

tyrant: someone who rules in a cruel way

Now it is 507 BC. Athens's leaders ask Cleisthenes to rebuild the government. Cleisthenes had helped defeat Hippias, and he has ideas for a new government. The people hope Cleisthenes's new government will give them a say in how they're ruled. But there is a chance that their new ruler will be another terrible tyrant.

Cleisthenes

Fighting in the Colonies

American colonists know what a tyrant's rule is like. And they are willing to fight against it. But winning the war against King George III is going to be hard—if not impossible. Most colonists are not trained soldiers. And they're fighting one of the best militaries in the world.

During the war, the Continental Congress forms a set of rules for the colonies to follow. The Articles of Confederation give individual states a lot of power. In fact it's almost like there are 13 different countries.

The Revolutionary War is a long, bloody war. Thousands of fighters lose their lives. Finally, on October 19, 1781, the ending scenes of the war unfold. Britain's General Charles Cornwallis surrenders to General George Washington. The impossible has just become possible. A ragtag army has defeated the most powerful nation in the world!

Now in 1787, the colonies are independent. But they are struggling to keep the new country together. Each state has its own laws and money. And the states are taxing citizens to pay huge war debts. Many people lose their land because they can't pay the taxes.

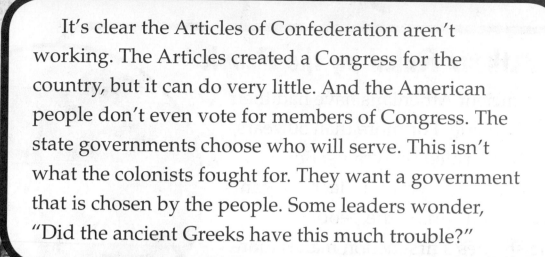

It's clear the Articles of Confederation aren't working. The Articles created a Congress for the country, but it can do very little. And the American people don't even vote for members of Congress. The state governments choose who will serve. This isn't what the colonists fought for. They want a government that is chosen by the people. Some leaders wonder, "Did the ancient Greeks have this much trouble?"

Battle at Guilford Courthouse

Making Democracies

An Athens Ruled by the People

The ancient Athenians have had their share of trouble. For more than 50 years, they've been ruled by tyrants. But Cleisthenes is no tyrant. In fact, he wants a government run by the people.

Cleisthenes's first action makes more free men citizens. Before this time, a man had to be born in the city to be a citizen. Now those born in the countryside are citizens too. Then Cleisthenes allows all citizens to be members of the Assembly. The Assembly is the city's lawmaking body. Every citizen—rich and poor—gets a vote here.

Assembly meetings occur on a hill outside Athens every 10 days. Thousands come to listen to speakers debate laws, wars, and taxes. No laws are made in Athens unless they are approved by the Assembly.

Cleisthenes also forms the Council of the Five Hundred to run the daily business of the city. Citizens draw lots to serve on the council. Being on the council gives citizens a chance to directly lead the government. Ideas for laws or taxes start in the council. Then the council brings ideas to the Assembly for a vote.

It has taken years for this day to come. But finally the people of Athens have what they fought for. They have a government ruled by the people!

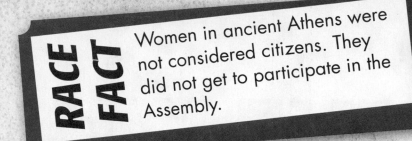
A Democratic America

A government ruled by the people is also becoming a reality in America. In May 1787, state leaders meet in Philadelphia to discuss a new plan for the country. The men use their knowledge of the past to guide their future. They discuss Solon, Cleisthenes, and the government of ancient Athens. They review the Magna Carta, a document that forced British kings to follow laws.

The leaders debate many issues. After four long months, they finally come to an agreement. Their new government will share power between the national and state governments. It will also divide power between judicial, executive, and legislative branches.

The leaders also decide to give people a voice in their government. Citizens won't vote for every law. They will vote for leaders who make the laws. If the people don't like how leaders act, they can vote them out.

Finally, the people have what they fought for. The United States is officially ruled by the people!

THE WINNER

Both players overcame many hurdles in the race for democracy. But it was the people of ancient Greece who were the winners. In 507 BC, the people of Athens formed a government they called a democracy, or people power. Today we call their government a direct democracy. In direct democracies citizens vote directly for laws.

The patriots in America created a government run by the people too. However, they weren't the first to do so. The Americans actually studied Athens's ancient democracy when they designed their government. Unlike the ancient Greeks, the Americans didn't allow citizens to vote for every law. But they did allow them to vote for representatives who could make laws for them. This type of government is called a representative democracy.

Many other nations have followed in the footsteps of the Greeks and Americans. Today more than 100 nations have democratic governments. People in other countries are fighting for a say in their governments. If you look at it in that way, the race for democracy continues today.

A More Perfect Union

THE STORY OF OUR CONSTITUTION

by Betsy and Giulio Maestro

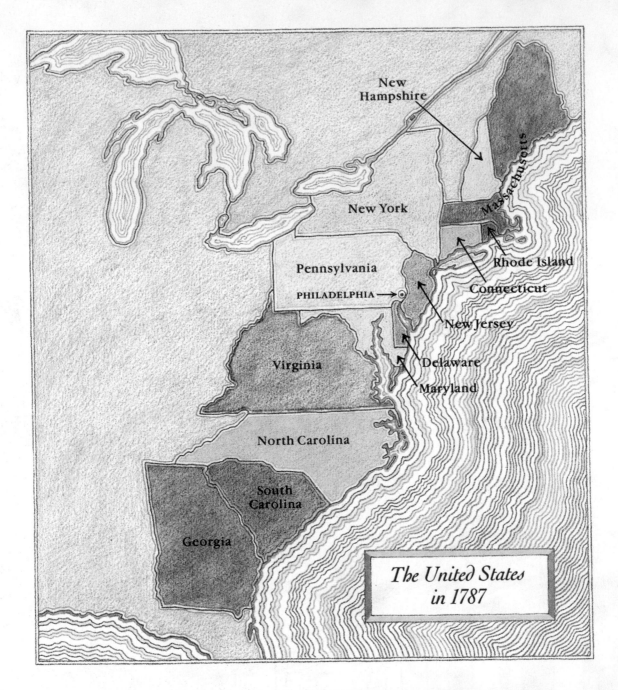

The United States in 1787

Two hundred years ago, America was still a very young country. Representatives from the thirteen colonies met in 1776 to write the Declaration of Independence, which told King George III of England that the colonies wanted to rule themselves. The colonists formed their own government and fought the Revolutionary War to win their freedom.

But ten years later, in 1786, America was in trouble. The government was not working well. Many people were poor. The thirteen states were not cooperating with one another. The government had no way to raise money, and there was no President to help the states work together as one nation.

The leaders of the new country were very worried and sad to see America in such trouble. They were afraid the country would fall apart if something was not done soon to make the government strong. These men decided to hold a special meeting, called a convention, to figure out what could be done. A few leaders from each state were invited to come to Philadelphia in May 1787.

Important men began arriving in Philadelphia. George Washington and James Madison came from Virginia. Alexander Hamilton was sent from New York, and Benjamin Franklin was there to speak for Pennsylvania. Many delegates stayed at the Indian Queen, one of the nicest inns.

Even before the convention began, the men were talking over their ideas and plans. Nearly all of them knew one another, as some of them had helped to write the Declaration of Independence, many had fought in the Revolutionary War, and most had served in the government. Now they were all anxious to help their country again.

The convention was to begin on May 14, but most of the delegates did not arrive by that date. Travel was very slow in those days. Some of the men came long distances by horseback, carriage, or ship.

The trip to Philadelphia from New Hampshire or Georgia could take two or three weeks. In addition, the weather was bad. Finally, by May 25, most of the delegates had arrived, and the convention began.

The convention took place in the State House on Chestnut Street. This building, which we now call Independence Hall, is where the Declaration of Independence had been signed eleven years before. At the very first meeting, the delegates voted to make George Washington the leader of the convention.

James Madison offered to write down everything that happened during the meetings, so there would be a record of all that was said and done. Even though the convention lasted for sixteen weeks, Madison did not miss a single meeting. His work was so important that he is called the Father of the Constitution.

When George Washington took his place at the desk on the platform, Benjamin Franklin noticed a sun carved on his chair. Franklin wondered whether it was a rising sun or a setting sun. He did not have much time to think about it, however, as the work of the convention had begun.

During the next few days, the men made a set of rules to help the convention run smoothly. Some of the rules were: each state would have one vote; a majority, or more than half the votes, would rule; and everything that happened at the meetings would be kept secret until after the convention was over.

Some of those who had arrived in Philadelphia early, including George Washington and James Madison, had come up with a plan to form a new government. Governor Edmund Randolph of Virginia presented this plan to the convention, so it became known as the Virginia Plan. The plan called for a government elected, or chosen, by the people. It would have three parts: a President, a congress or a group of people to make laws, and a law court to make decisions about those laws.

Each state would choose delegates to serve in Congress. The number of delegates from each state would depend on the size of the state. This meant that big states would have more power than small states because they would have more votes in Congress.

Many of the delegates were very surprised by the
Virginia Plan. They thought the convention would fix
up the old government, not make a new one. They had
to decide. Should they create a new government for
America?

They took a vote and the yeses won. Now the job of the
convention would be to write a constitution, a set of rules
for forming a government, and another set of rules for the
new government to follow.

Right away the delegates began to argue. The members from small states thought the Virginia Plan was unfair. They wanted each state to have the same number of representatives. Other delegates were afraid to let the people choose the President. They felt that ordinary citizens would make a bad choice. The delegates argued for weeks.

Finally, some members from the small states came up with a plan of their own called the New Jersey Plan. It said that, except for some small changes, the old government was fine. The most important thing the New Jersey Plan said was that all the states, no matter what their size, would have the same number of representatives.

After a few days of talking, the majority voted against the New Jersey Plan. The delegates from small states had lost their fight, and were bitterly disappointed, but they decided to work with the other delegates to come up with a plan that would satisfy both large and small states. By mid-July, with the help of some delegates from Connecticut, a compromise was worked out. Each side had given up something it wanted in order to create a plan that both sides could accept. The plan was called the Great Compromise or the Connecticut Compromise. It was made up of some parts of the Virginia Plan, some parts of the New Jersey Plan, and some new ideas from both sides.

That summer in Philadelphia was hot, and the men were very tired. Most of them took some time now for a short vacation. They saw the sights of the city and enjoyed their free days. Some of them borrowed books from the library that Benjamin Franklin had started years before.

However, a small group of delegates called the Committee of Detail did not take a vacation. They gathered together all the parts of the new plan for the Constitution and wrote a first draft, or working copy. When the whole group of fifty-five delegates returned to the convention, they were able to look over this draft of the document that would govern all the American people.

On August 6, the delegates began to examine the draft of the new Constitution. Every sentence was argued, debated, and discussed by the members of the convention. By the end of the month, the delegates had agreed on almost everything. Again, the spirit of compromise saved the day.

Then another committee, the Committee of Style and Arrangement, went to work. Its members rewrote the final draft, making sure that every word was just right. At last, the Constitution was complete. Copies were printed and given to the delegates.

On September 15, the delegates voted to sign the new Constitution. Forty-two members were present, and only three did not agree to sign. Then the words were copied onto parchment, a very special kind of paper that lasts for a long time.

On Monday, September 17, 1787, the convention had its final meeting. Thirty-nine delegates signed the new Constitution. Some of the original fifty-five delegates had left the convention in anger because they did not approve of the new Constitution. Some others would have signed, but had to return home early.

111

The signing of the Constitution was a formal ceremony. George Washington was the first to write his name. Then the other thirty-eight men followed. Although it was a serious and important moment, it was also a very happy one.

Ben Franklin commented that at last he knew for sure what kind of sun was on Washington's chair—it was a rising sun! Everyone felt this was a good sign for the rising young country. Now all the men were anxious to get home. Many had not seen their families for months.

Much hard work still lay ahead. The Constitution had to be ratified, or approved, in each state before it could become law. The delegates had to convince the people in their home states to vote for the new Constitution.

Copies were sent to all the state governments. Each of the thirteen states would hold its own convention to vote. If nine of the thirteen states, or a two-thirds majority, voted for the new Constitution, the new government would be set up.

Many people were in favor of the new Constitution and many were against it. Those who didn't like it were afraid the new government would be too strong—that living in America would be much the same as living under English rule. The debates in the states went on, and in December 1787, Delaware became the first state to approve the new Constitution. Pennsylvania, New Jersey, Georgia, and Connecticut quickly followed. Massachusetts came next in February 1788, after a very close vote in the state convention. By June, after Maryland and South Carolina had ratified, eight states had agreed to the new government.

Now only one more state was needed for the new Constitution to become law. On June 21, 1788, New Hampshire voted yes. America would have a new government. The state of Virginia soon ratified as well.

When July 4 came, huge celebrations were held in many cities. In New York, a big ship was pulled through the streets in a parade. In Philadelphia, there was a parade made up of eighty-eight groups of marchers, some on floats.

New York State soon accepted the new Constitution. A date was set for the first election, by the people, of a President of the United States. George Washington was everyone's choice; he was elected by unanimous vote. On April 30, 1789, he took the oath of office, promising to serve his country well. Finally, by May 1790, all thirteen states had ratified the Constitution. Now the new nation could truly be called the United States of America.

A new Congress was elected, and it immediately went to work. Law courts were set up, and the new government seemed strong and sound.

But still some Americans worried. They believed that certain important rights of the people were not protected under the Constitution. So, to ease these fears, Congress proposed some additions to the Constitution.

The first ten additions, or amendments, are known as the Bill of Rights. In part, they state that people have the right to say what they want, go where they want, and pray to God in the way they want, without fear that the government will stop them. The Bill of Rights has turned out to be a very important part of the Constitution. It protects people from losing the freedom that is so much a part of American life.

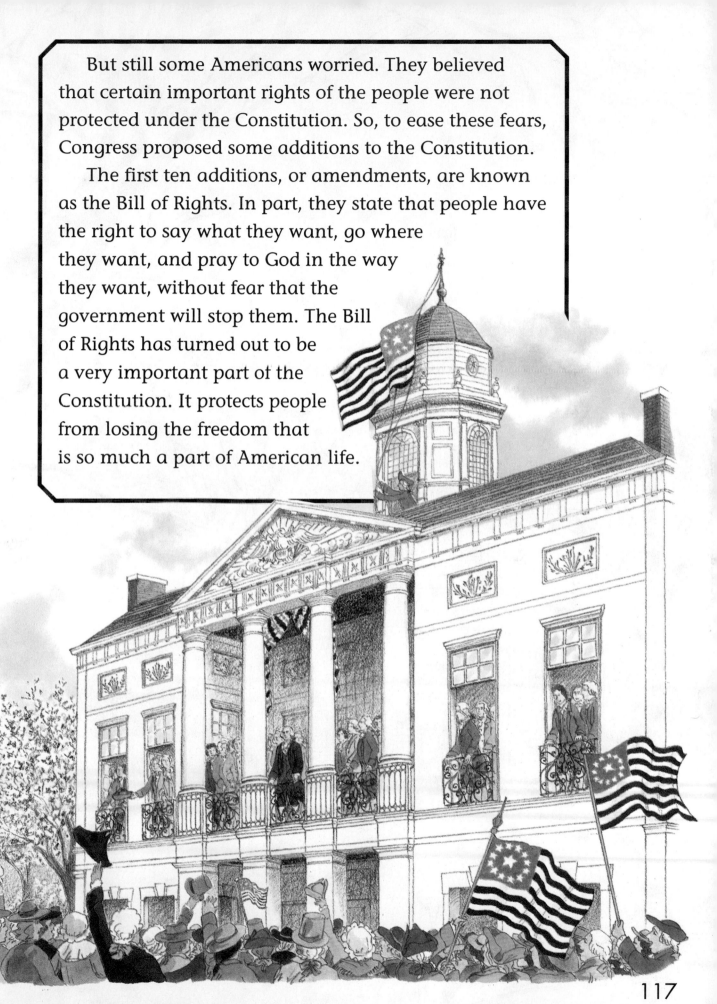

Over the years, sixteen other amendments have been added. Our Constitution was written so that, as times change, it can change to meet the needs of our growing country.

Today, some two hundred years after it was written, the Constitution is still the basis of American government and the American people's way of life. It is the oldest written set of rules for running a country still in use in the world. It created a government that has worked better and longer than any other in history.

The Founding Fathers, as the authors of the Constitution are called, wrote the Constitution with the idea that the power of government should come from the people. This idea of each citizen playing a part in government is one of the principles that makes America strong. Power from the people, protected and guaranteed by the Constitution, has kept a union of states, now grown to fifty, together all these years.

ROSA PARKS
HERO OF OUR TIME

by Garnet Nelson Jackson

In 1955, Rosa Parks and her husband were living in Montgomery, Alabama. She had a job sewing clothes.

One day after work she boarded a bus to go home. The bus became crowded.

When a white man got on the bus, there were no empty seats, so the bus driver told Rosa to give up her seat.

Rosa knew this was not fair. So with bravery and dignity, she said very softly, "No."

The police were called. Rosa was arrested and taken to jail. This was December 1, 1955.

Rosa was released that night. But four days later, she had to stand trial.

Black people became very angry about this. Some white people were angry, too. They knew Rosa was right.

African Americans throughout Montgomery decided they would not ride the buses the day of

the trial. Instead, they walked and they gave each other rides. They continued doing this for a whole year. This was called the Montgomery Bus Boycott.

Finally, the United States Supreme Court, the highest court in the nation, said that Rosa was right. African Americans could sit anywhere they wanted to on the buses. And they did not have to give their seats to white people. So, the boycott ended.

Rosa Parks's bravery helped make life better for all Americans.

Brother Against Brother

by Patricia J. Murphy

It was . . .
North against South . . .
Brother against Brother . . .
Blue against Gray . . .
One against another . . .
Loyal soldiers . . .
Marching into battle . . .
Standing tall . . .
Looking into the enemy's eyes . . .
Seeing a brother . . .
A father . . .
A friend . . .
Another . . .
Looking back at them . . .
And, for a moment . . .
Did they remember?
Did they recall?
Marching together . . .
When they were small?
Fighting make-believe battles
With make-believe guns . . .
Until it was dark
Under the sun . . .
Or . . .
Until their mothers called them in . . .
For mealtime . . .
For bedtime . . .
And their battles
Would wait . . .
For another time . . .
For another day . . .
A day . . .
No one dreamt would ever come . . .
No one . . .
No way . . .

The Little Black-Eyed Rebel

by Will Carleton

A boy drove into the city, his wagon loaded down
With food to feed the people of the British-governed town;
And the little black-eyed rebel, so innocent and sly,
Was watching for his coming from the corner of her eye.

His face looked broad and honest, his hands were brown and tough;
The clothes he wore upon him were homespun, coarse and rough;
But one there was who watched him, who long time lingered nigh,
And cast at him sweet glances from the corner of her eye.

He drove up to the market, he waited in the line,
His apples and potatoes were fresh and fair and fine
But long and long he waited, and no one came to buy
Save the black-eyed rebel, watching from the corner of her eye.

"Now who will buy my apples?" he shouted, long and loud;
And "Who wants my potatoes?" he repeated to the crowd;
But from all the people round him came no word of a reply,
Save the black-eyed rebel, answering from the corner of her eye.

For she knew that 'neath the lining of the coat he wore that day,
Were long letters from the husbands and the fathers far away,
Who were fighting for the freedom that they meant to gain or die;
And a tear like silver glistened in the corner of her eye.

But the treasures—how to get them? crept the question through her
    mind,
Since keen enemies were watching for what prizes they might find;
And she paused a while and pondered, with a pretty little sigh;
Then resolve crept through her features, and a shrewdness fired her eye.

So she resolutely walked up to the wagon old and red;
"May I have a dozen apples for a kiss?" she sweetly said.
And the brown face flushed to scarlet, for the boy was somewhat shy,
And he saw her laughing from the corner of her eye.

"You may have them all for nothing, and more, if you want," said he.
"I will have them, my good fellow, but I'll pay for them," said she;
And she clambered on the wagon, minding not who all were by,
With a laugh of reckless romping in the corner of her eye.

Clinging round his brawny neck, she clasped her fingers white and small,
And then whispered, "Quick! the letters! thrust them underneath
    my shawl!
Carry back again *this* package, and be sure that you are spry!"
And she sweetly smiled upon him from the corner of her eye.

Loud the motley crowd were laughing at the strange, ungirlish freak,
And the boy was scared and panting, and so dashed he could not speak;
And, "Miss, *I* have good apples," a bolder lad did cry;
But she answered, "No, I thank you," from the corner of her eye.

With the news of loved ones absent to the dear friends they would greet,
Searching them who hungered for them, swift she glided through
    the street.
"There is nothing worth the doing that it does not pay to try,"
Thought the little black-eyed rebel, with a twinkle in her eye.

DARE

by Laura Purdie Salas

Dare to say
Race does not matter and
Each person can do
Amazing things. This is
MY DREAM!

WHERE?

by Eleanor Roosevelt

Where after all do human rights begin?
In small places close to home
   Such are the places
Where every man, woman and child
   Seeks equal justice
   Equal opportunity
   Equal dignity

America

by Samuel Francis Smith

My country, 'tis of thee,
Sweet land of liberty,
Of thee I sing;
Land where my fathers died,
Land of the Pilgrim's pride,
From ev'ry mountainside
Let freedom ring!

My native country, thee,
Land of the noble free,
Thy name I love;
I love thy rocks and rills,
Thy woods and templed hills;
My heart with rapture thrills,
Like that above.

Let music swell the breeze,
And ring from all the trees
Sweet freedom's song.
Let mortal tongues awake;
Let all that breathe partake;
Let rocks their silence break,
The sound prolong.

Washington, D.C.

by Rebecca Kai Dotlich

On the east bank of the Potomac,
lies Washington, D.C.
the capital of our Nation
which stands for liberty.

It's here our U.S. Presidents
are sworn into command;
where the courtly U.S. Capitol
and the stately White House stand.

Sweet cherry blossoms spice the air
of city blocks in patterned squares,
and grassy knolls and splendid parks
claim rare museums and grand landmarks.

Where patriotic monuments
stand haunting in the night;
where King proclaimed, *I have a dream,*
and Kennedy's flame burns bright.

It's here, in a place called Arlington,
where stars and stripes do fly;
where silent snow-white tombstones march
in rows where heroes lie.

The Tomb of the Unknown Soldier;
the changing of the guard.
The gardens and the galleries,
the tree-lined boulevards.

From around the world they come to touch
with tears and hushed acclaim
the sleek and sacred granite Wall
engraved with soldiers' names.

On the east bank of the Potomac,
lies Washington, D.C.
the capital of our Nation
which stands for liberty.

Text

Knots on a Counting Rope © Text copyright 1987 by Bill Martin Jr. and John Archambault. Illustrations © by Ted Rand. Reprinted by permission of Henry Holt & Company, LLC. All Rights Reserved.

"Paul Bunyan" by Stephen Krensky and illustrated by Craig Orback. Text copyright © 2007 by Stephen Krensky. Illustrations copyright © 2007 by Craig Orback. Reprinted with the permission of Millbrook Press, a division of Lerner Publishing Group, Inc. All rights reserved. No part of this excerpt may be used or reproduced in any manner whatsoever without the prior written permission of Lerner Publishing Group, Inc.

On the Same Day in March by Marilyn Singer, illustrations by Frané Lessac. Copyright © 2000. Used by permission of HarperCollins Publishers.

Typical Temperatures chart. Courtesy of mathisfun.com

"Tools for Measuring Weather," from Scott Foresman Grade 3 Interactive Science. Copyright © 2013 Pearson Education, Inc., or its affiliates. Used by permission. All Rights Reserved.

"Where Would You Be?" Copyright © 1964, renewed by Karla Kuskin. Reprinted by permission of S©ott Treimel NY.

"Storm," copyright © 1965 by Adrien Stoutenberg. Copyright renewed 1992 by Laura Nelson Baker. First appeared in *The Things That Are,* published by Contemporary Books. Reprinted by permission of Curtis Brown, Ltd.

"The Wind," © James Reeves from *Complete Poems for Children* (Heinemann).

"Tornado Season," copyright © 1965 by Adrien Stoutenberg. Copyright renewed 1992 by Laura Nelson Baker. First appeared in *The Things That Are,* published by Contemporary Books. Reprinted by permission of Curtis Brown, Ltd.

Back of the Bus. Text copyright © 2010 by Aaron Reynolds, illustration copyright © 2010 by Floyd Cooper. Used by permission of Penguin Young Readers, A Member of Penguin Group (USA) Inc., 345 Hudson Street, New York, NY 10014. All rights reserved.

"Who Really Created Democracy?" Excerpted from the work entitled *Who Really Created Democracy?* © 2011 by Capstone. All rights reserved.

A More Perfect Union by Betsy Maestro. Text copyright © 1987 by Betsy Maestro. Illustrations copyright © 1987 by Giulio Maestro. Used by permission of HarperCollins Publishers.

"Rosa Parks: Hero of Our Time," from *Rosa Parks: Hero of Our Time* by Garnet Jackson. Copyright © 1993 Pearson Education, Inc., or its affiliates. Used by permission. All Rights Reserved.

"Brother Against Brother," from *Appleseeds* issue: *Growing Up in the Civil War,* © 2003 Carus Publishing Company, published by Cobblestone Publishing, 30 Grove Street, Suite C, Peterborough, NH 03458. All Rights Reserved. Used by permission of the publisher. www.cobblestonepub.com

"The Little Black-Eyed Rebel." Carleton, Will. *Poems for Young Americans.* New York: NY: Harper & Row, 1906.

"Dare," excerpted from the work entitled: *Tiny Dreams, Sprouting Tall* © 2008 by Capstone. All rights reserved.

"Where?" From *Hour of Freedom: History in Poetry,* edited by Milton Meltzer. Copyright © 2003 by Milton Meltzer. Published by Wordsong, an imprint of Boyds Mills Press. Reprinted by permission.

"Washington, D.C." Copyright © 2000 by Rebecca Kai Dotlich. Published in *My America: A Poetry Atlas of the United States,* selected by Lee Bennett Hopkins, published by Simon & Schuster. Reprinted by permission of Curtis Brown, Ltd.

Illustrations

60–64 Anita & Andrzej

Photographs

Photo locators denoted as follows: Top (T), Center (C), Bottom (B), Left (L), Right (R), Background (Bkgd)

6 ©marina_ua/Shutterstock; 25 Thomas Rossiter; 80 The Granger Collection; 81 (Bkgd) ©Svetlana Kuznetsova/Shutterstock, (BR) Superstock/Superstock, (TL) Bridgeman Art Library, (TR) Anna Christoforidis; 82 ©Svetlana Kuznetsova/Shutterstock; 83 (Bkgd) ©Larisa Koshkina/Shutterstock, (T) SuperStock; 84 Bridgeman Art Library; 85 (B) Library of Congress, (T) Bridgeman Art Library; 89 Bridgeman Art Library; 90 SuperStock; 95 Army Art Collection/US Army Center of Military History/Bridgeman Art Library; 120 ©Pictorial Press Ltd/Alamy; 121 ©GL Archive/Alamy; 122 (T) ©kuleczka/Shutterstock, (Bkgd) ©Associated Press; 124 (B) ©Stock Montage/Contributor/Archive Photos/Getty Images, (T) Library of Congress, Prints & Photographs Division, U.S. News & World Report Magazine Collection, LC-U9-10361, frame 15; 125 ©Images Etc Ltd/Photographer's Choice RF/Getty Images; 127 Shutterstock.